If Tits Could Talk

By Holly McComish

Illustrations by Nadine Kaur

Holly McComish (She/Her) is a UK based writer and poet whose work was discovered by Rupi Kaur in 2020. Holly performed her poem *If Tits Could Talk* live on Rupi's Instagram to over 4 million followers. Blown away by the worldwide response, Holly has since performed the poem for The Pink Ribbon Foundation's breast cancer awareness advert and live at the charity's 25th anniversary ball. Holly's debut collection focuses on women's health issues.

holly_mccomish

Acknowledgements

Brunel University

Lara McComish

Leila Lufti

Purple Moon Drama

Royal Court Theatre

Santander

Steve McComish & team at Motive PR

The Pink Ribbon Foundation

Nadine Kaur (she/her) is the illustrator. A UK based artist, specialising in mixed media landscapes and fantasy realism. She has recently begun exploring digital art and illustration.

For all the women in my life x

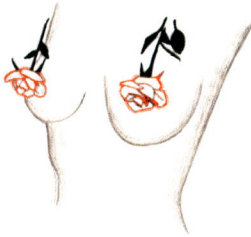

(....And my Dad) x

Contents

If Tits Could Talk

If tits could talk, what would they say?
If boobs could speak for just one day...

Stop wearing those bras that are falling to pieces!
(Sorry for stretching your best shirts and fleeces)

Stop pushing us together, Christ we need air!
Believe us when we say, it gets sweaty down there

So when you next go running
Or fancy something sporty,
Don't forget your friends down here
Might need some more support-y

Stop worrying about whether we look round and perky!
(All tits sag by the age of 30)

We may sit apart
We may look down
We each have a nose
Either pink or brown

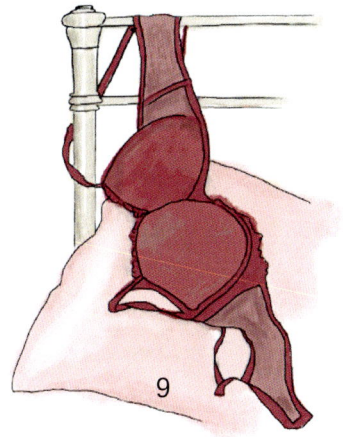

We're all slightly different
That's Mother Nature's aim
For how boring it'd be
To all look the same?

So stop squashing us down
To make us look smaller
Wear us with pride!
Stand a little taller

And even if we're slightly smaller
This needn't be an issue
For size does not define a woman
Nor do pads or tissue

If tits could talk, I'm sure they'd say
Fuck, it's bloody cold today!
And why does he keep staring?
Is it because of what we're wearing?

All these eyes are glaring
We really wish they'd stop
For you miss a woman's face
When you're talking to her top

If tits could talk, I'm sure they'd say
Love us please, in every way!
Buy us bras that fit just right
Hold us tightly through the night

When you bleed each month,
Remember, we're sore!
So allow us to relax
Drop the bras to the floor

And just know it's ok
To wear tops that reveal
Because YOU decide
Who cops a feel

Know your bust is more than lust,
This assumption very wrong
For one day, we could feed children
To make them big and strong

There's one last thing we must get off our chest,
To say it now I think it's best

Please, you have to check us
Don't make it such a chore
Always feel for lumps and bumps
That were not there before.

If tits could talk, I'd want them to say
Look after us, we're important x

A Poem To My Period

On the loo
I wait for you
With knickers round my feet
You're running late to see me
So I warm the toilet seat

Never a timely lady
Likes to keep me on my toes
Always has me guessing
When she'll come and when she'll go

She can rock up without warning
Just burst in without a care
If I bloody had some notice
I'd change my good underwear!

Sore nips, breasts heavy
Trapped wind in a bloated belly
Mood swinging, head aching

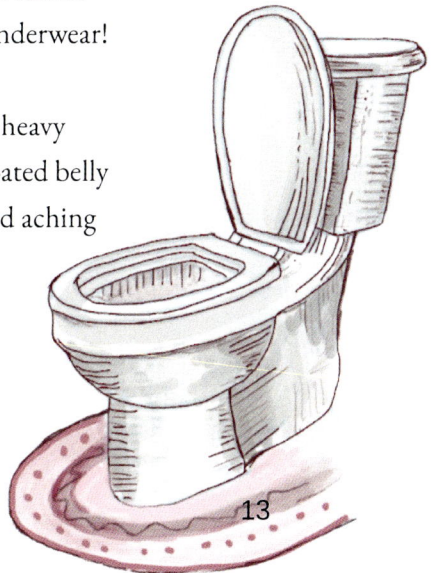

13

Greasy hair and skin that's breaking
Surely you must be on your way??
It's been too long!
Please come today.

Left to wait
I contemplate
A few of my decisions
The meet and greets
Between the sheets
With no use of... provisions

Once or twice is fine though, right?
In the heat of having fun
Forgetting contraception
Flying closer to the sun

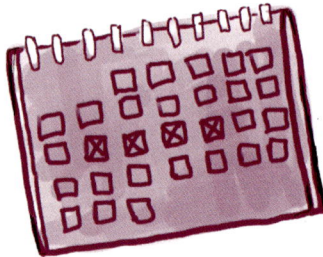

Must not panic
(I'm not PaNicKiNg?)
She's never let me down before
Always comes eventually
In her crimson red couture

But it's been a full 6 days now
Since she said that she'd be here
I desperately search between my legs
And hope that she'll appear

(One day, it won't be like this
In fact, I'll beg her not to come
I'll pray to God I'll miss her
So that I can be a mum)

But right now, I'm just not there yet
My bank card's about to give
I still live in a flatshare
And have more selfish nights to live

I promise to be more careful
As I go to bed with men
No more *just this once's*
Or *just the tip* again

But right now I really need you
To make these worries go away
I'd also like to leave the loo
And crack on with my day

Please hurry x

Down There

Something twitchy, kind of itchy
Is coming from down there
A funny smells begins to dwell
From inside my underwear

With legs crossed on the chair
Of a packed out train
I must contain
My fanny's feelings

But the itching's getting stronger
It grows hard to keep concealing

Could try rubbing on the seat?
Is that discrete?
(Turns out it's not)
Plus now that old man's staring
I think he might've found that hot?

Got to find the nearest toilet
Please sir MOVE I'm in a rush
No one wants to be in public
With a nasty case of thrush x

The Nurse Will See You Now

Eyes to the floor
Then on the door
How many more before it's me?
(Hardly your finest moment
Getting checked for STDs)

The air's filled with anxiety
And hair removal cream
The receptionist scoffs
At occasional coughs
And requests of when you'll be seen:

Couldn't tell you!!
Hard to say!!!
We've only got one nurse today!!!

Passive aggressive posters
Can't help but catch your eye
LOTS of sexual partners???
Best give condoms a try!! :)

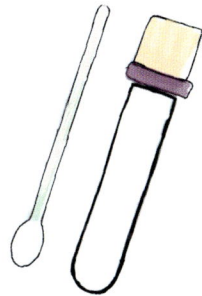

I sigh as the guy
Sitting opposite
Has his hands shoved down his trousers
Scratching very vigorously
Making minutes feel like hours

I await my fate
At the mercy of the nurse
(REALLY must remember
To put those condoms in my purse)

What's worse is I'm sat holding
A small cup of my own piss
Dark and cloudy yellow
(She's a dehydrated sis)

They say ignorance is bliss
But it's always best to go
To get yourself checked out
When certain symptoms start to show

(Plus STIs are sneaky
Some you'll have and never know!)
Our fannies deserve better
And getting checked is completely free
STIs, if left untreated
Can cause us infertility x

Growing Pains

There comes an age, we reach this stage
Where we're sort of stuck in between
(Like a packet of crisps that won't quite fall from its slot in
the vending machine)

Like we're holding on to something
Scared to take the dive
To pay back Miss Student Finance
With a solid 9 to 5

For the shops to still ID us
You sure you don't wanna see?
(It's hard not to get offended
When you're only 23)

That's not old, so I'm told
By older men online
But why does it feel so late to put a film on after 9?

It's when you still enjoy a drink
(Especially if it's free)
But it's less socially accepted
To be passed out by a tree

See, now that behaviour's worrying
Friends ask *Is everything alright?*
But before it made you a legend
A Jäger warrior of the night

It's when half of Facebook's married
With a new house, car or baby

Whilst the other half still lives at home
And will learn to drive next year... maybe
It's when your CV has experience and a bachelor's degree
But you still feel about a million miles
From where you want to be

It's when you've travelled to great places
But have so much more to cover
It's the pressure to achieve your dreams
Before you're someone's mother

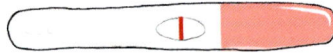

It's wanting something different
But being scared to make the change
It's the gap between a salary and an hourly wage
It's being old enough to know better
But still young enough to leap
It's these constant growing pains
As we try to find our feet x

Sporty Chic

Too many girls have walked away
From sports they've always loved to play
Chubby nips
Sweaty pits
Wider hips
And hair below

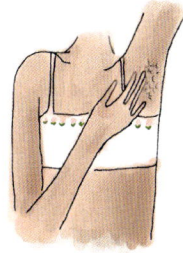

Bodies changing
Rearranging
We find reasons not to go
To P.E lessons
And sports days
Scared of how
Our breasts may show

We grow taller
Yet feel smaller
Mocked for how
We catch and throw

We don't know
How to swim
With tampons in?
As swimsuits cling
Tighter to our skin

Hormones racing
Thighs start chafing
Confidence shrinking
Gets girls thinking
Perhaps it's time to pack this in

Young girls in sport
Need more support
To push through puberty
Most reach the age
Then disengage
A sight so sad to see

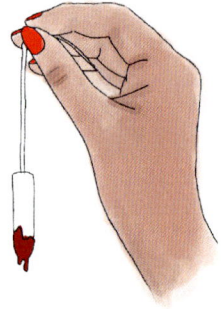

For sport is linked to
Our self worth
Assurance
And esteem
To body positivity
And working as a team

We also need more female athletes on our TV screens!
The Kelly Holmes
Emma Raducanus
And Paula Radcliffes too
The Alex Scotts
Laura Kennys
(Just to name a few!)

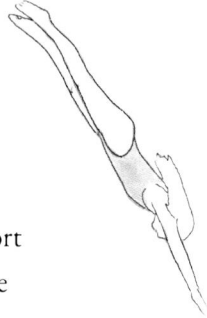

So let's support young girls in sport
When going through this change
To give advice on periods
So that they seem less strange

To give girls chances like the boys
For this is their space too
Girls need more opportunities
To show what they can do x

Smear Fear

25, a letter arrives
An invitation just for you
Not to a party, or a wedding
But your first smear test that's due

Written in bold, you're firmly told
To book in with your GP
We're testing for abnormal cells
So best get seen quickly

They might as well write CANCER
As that's where your mind will go
Plus you'll have to take your pants off
For a woman you don't know

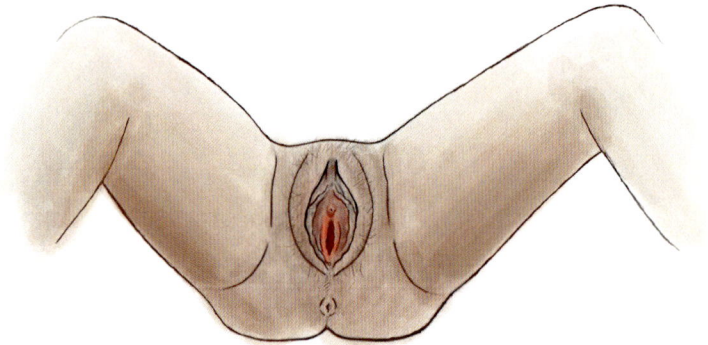

And you've only *just* turned 25
So really what's the hurry?
You shove the letter in a drawer
And see no need to worry

But as time goes by
The smear fear grows
The longer you wait
The more it shows

Just too busy, got no time!
I'll sort it further down the line

Someone like me doesn't need to be seen
I've had the HPV vaccine!

Final reminders through your door
Perhaps you should have gone before
Your smear fear gained her power
She'll convince you not to go
That it's better not to know
So the taste of it is sour

What she'll fail to say
Is the more you delay
The more harm you could be causing
For it's not a test for cancer
But a test to stop it forming

That the test takes just 2 minutes
Then you're on your merry way
(Your fanny's nothing special
To a nurse seeing hundreds a day)

So there *really* is no need to shave
Just get yourself booked in
For to be scared is to be brave
Don't let the smear fear win x

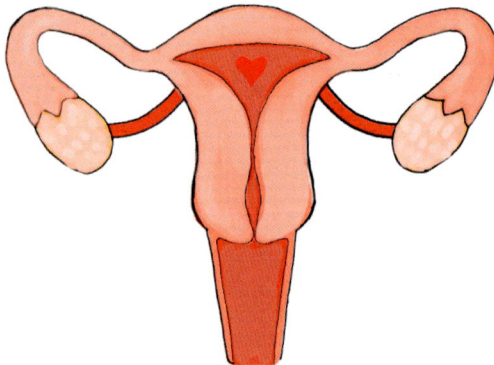

Bloody Mary Shag

The best sex is always messy
But when you're on your rag
There's something *extra* filthy
In a Bloody Mary Shag

Too horny to care
About stained sheets
We just ride that crimson tide
Til our orgasms meet

It's never discrete
But with hormones on the rise
The only way to ease my cramps
Is you between my thighs

So let's throw down a towel
Or take things to the shower
Itches still need scratching
We can make it happy hour x

To Pill Or Not To Pill?

There's a common misconception
When it comes to contraception
Despite the vast selection
What's my best form of protection?

Pills, patches
Coils and sharp scratches
Implants and injections
Or wrapping up erections?

In this sexual revolution
Birth control is our solution
To shaking the sheets without care
Of a pregnancy scare

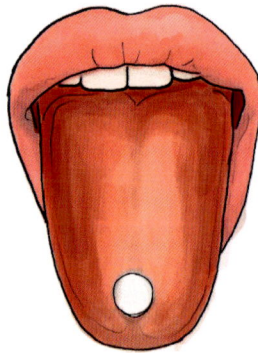

So which one should I choose?
What option is best for me?
And how does each one work?
(Not taught this stuff in school, you see)

Instead we're left to Google
Which method might be best
Or ask our GP nurse
To give an educated guess

Don't stress!
Though some side effects are scary
We're promised by a pamphlet
That they happen very rarely

Plus women now thrive
With the power to decide
Their own destinies

To be breadwinners
Business owners
Doctors, Dentists galore

Leading lives our grandmas
Could once only dream for
And that's all thanks to birth control
One of women's greatest wins

(I'm still not sure which one's for me)
But contraception? Count me in x

Poppin' Pills

It's summer '21
My first pack's begun
And so far, I'm feeling ok
But I do keep getting headaches
And my periods gone away

Goodbye to pads and tampons!
(I guess really that's a plus)
But last week I felt so dizzy
Just when standing on the bus

I assume this all is normal
That side effects will come in stages
When you change your body's natural flow
You're bound to feel some changes

So I swill the pill each morning
Just like many women do
Taking comfort in the fact that
They might feel this too

Except now it's Halloween
And something scary starts to happen
The room has started spinning
And my mind begins to blacken

My body cannot move
And my eyes they cannot see
All sound has disappeared
And half my face has sunk from me

Why is this happening?
What is it that I've done?
An ambulance is called
While a stranger rings my mum

Paramedics arrive
And I can hear this kind Welsh bloke
Who tells me
Not to panic, but we think you've had a stroke x

What Doesn't Pill You Makes You Stronger

A stroke?
Is this a joke?
But I'm only 25
Just moved into my new flat
And started learning how to drive
A stroke?
I choke
This surely can't be real
I'm a member of the gym
And eat some veg with every meal?
I feel old as I'm told
To start daily medication
New pills to thin my blood
That will help with circulation
Told to stop the birth control
As it's caused my blood to clot
A serious side effect
That no one speaks about a lot

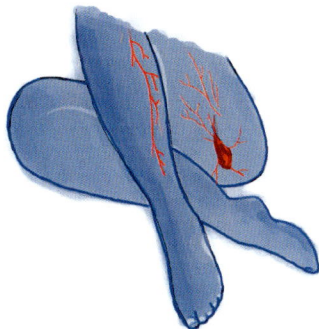

There's a common misconception
When it comes to contraception
Despite the vast selection
Young women need more direction
In understanding how protection
Works in many different ways
Containing different hormones not all bodies will obey

That family histories can't be mysteries
As they often are the clue
To which ones will suit you best
And which ones just aren't for you

Upon reflecting, when selecting
I should have thought about this longer
But women hear my story
And remember
What doesn't pill you makes you stronger x

A Quiet Moment

When I've got a quiet moment
There's nothing I love more
Than slipping off my pants
And reaching for the bedside drawer

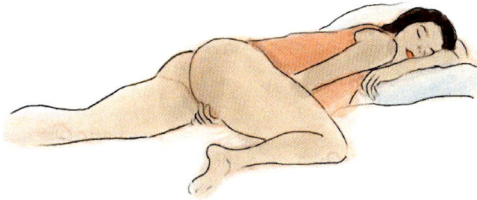

When I've got a quiet moment
You'll find me sprawled out on the bed
Eyes shut, unleashing fantasies
That live inside my head

When I've got a quiet moment
I like to spend some time
Exploring all my crevices
(My God, they feel *divine*)

When I've got a quiet moment
And need time to destress
Nothing does the job quite like
A simple self caress

With no pressure to impress
(Or even undress)
In a party just for you

We can see to our needs
However we please
(Making sure we finish too!)

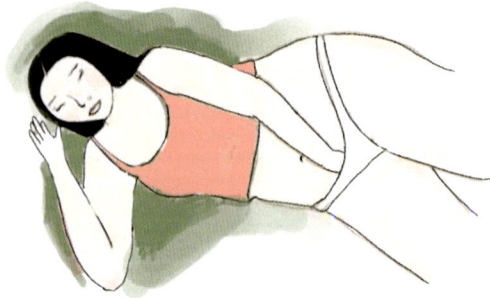

Not only does it feel good
But it helps us get to know
The bodies that we live in
And what excites them down below

Yet there's still some hesitation
Around female masturbation
Such a natural stimulation
Kept to whispered conversations

In school, it's ALL boys spoke about
Weekend wanks and balls being blue
Us girls, we kept things to ourselves
Like we're so often taught to do

A healthy human habit
Shouldn't have to hide in shame
Plus it can help us fall asleep
Or ease bad menstrual pains

With so many gains
This calls for champagne!
A toast to female pleasure
Here's to being proud
Of 'quiet moments'
And to our dildos that we treasure x

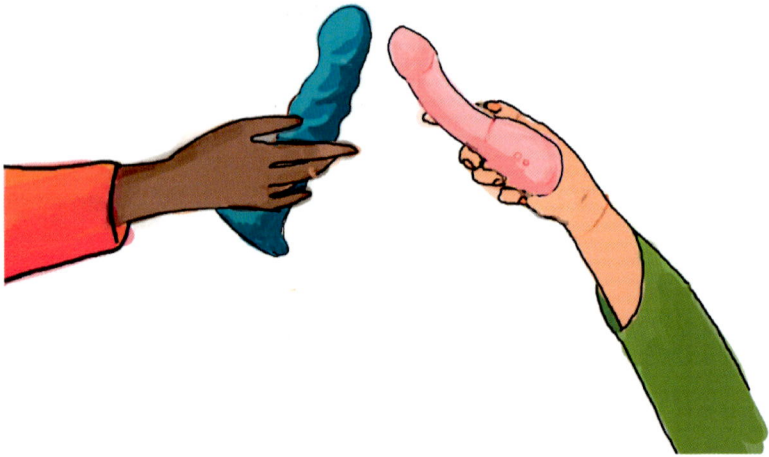

Cystitis Crisis

Dashing for a slash
(God, I *really* need to go)
I've got that funny feeling
One too many of us know

When pissing feels like fires
Burnt your bladder up in flames
Now I'm downing cranberry sachets
Praying that they ease the pain

Stranded on the toilet
For the feeling's just too strong
Everytime I leave
I'm crawling back not after long

(With patience thinner than my thong)
I can't stop myself from crying
I start work in half an hour
And I *think* I might be dying?

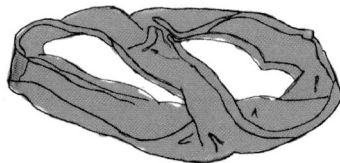

To top it off, he's not replying
Has my Whatsapps left on read
He's left you with this UTI
And fucked off back to bed

Oh how different things would be
If I'd just gotten up to wee
To flush out what's inside of me
Before I went to sleep

See, we've got to keep on top of this
It's for our own protection
Untreated UTIs can lead to
Serious infections x

Something's Wrong With Mum

Something's wrong with mum
She's not herself today
Flustered and forgetful
She seems lost for things to say

Something's wrong with mum
She's been in a right old mood
Doesn't want to go to work
And is on and off her food

Something's wrong with mum
She's just bought some red hair dye?
I'm trying something new!
She snaps at me when I ask why

She's stopped stocking tampons
In our bathroom drawer
Says I'll have to buy my own
For she won't need them anymore

Something's wrong with mum
At night I hear her crying
Can't sleep for her sheets seep with sweat
(She'll deny this, but she's lying)

She lies in dark rooms
With cold flannels on her head
And randomly at 2pm
She'll take herself to bed

She's hot and she's cold
And keeps running to the loo
When I ask what's wrong, she smiles and says
One day you'll feel this too

Something's wrong with mum
Says she's going through some changes
(I hope they finish soon
She's been like this for bloody ages!)

Yet over time
I start to see
The biggest change in mum
She's finally joined the gym
And signed up for that 10k run

She's started singing
Writing
Painting
Dancing
(Just to name a few)
All the things
She's always loved
But said she'd never do

Although the change was hard
One that women must see through
Since mum's crossed the finish line
It's made her feel brand new x

Drunk Queens

When I drink
I like to think
That I'm unstoppable

Proseccos pop
And I can't stop
Anything's possible!

There's no dance floor I can't conquer
Or cocktail I won't try
No spirit I can't master
Make them doubles, don't be shy!

I'll fly across the room
Singing loudly as I go
(Work's calling in the morning
But nobody needs to know)

For I'm sat in the loo
After a gin or two
Oversharing what I'm wearing
Befriending girls just passing through

No clue where my purse is
Whole bag's scattered round the bar
Jägers bomb inside me
As I smoke some blokes cigar

My flat is far from where we are
And I've just missed the last train back
I stumble in a chicken shop
To grab a late night snack

Tequilas sinked
I start to think
Of how I will get home
An Uber's out of the question
With the charge left on my phone

Alone.
I wander
With cheesy chips
Down darkened strips

Trying to find my quickest way
Keeping to myself
Just want to make it home okay

My Captain Morgan's confidence
Begins to quickly fade
As heckles hurl from passing cars
I walk frightened and afraid

See dark shadows wait to pray
On women walking late at night
Seizing opportunities
Once we step out the light

(Please be careful my drunk queens
When you are heading home tonight)

For they might not be a threat
But they'll always be a fear
When many girls just walking home
Forever disappear x